Latin Cuisine

A Latin Cookbook with Delicious Latin and South American Recipes

By
BookSumo Press

Published by
http://www.booksumo.com

Table of Contents

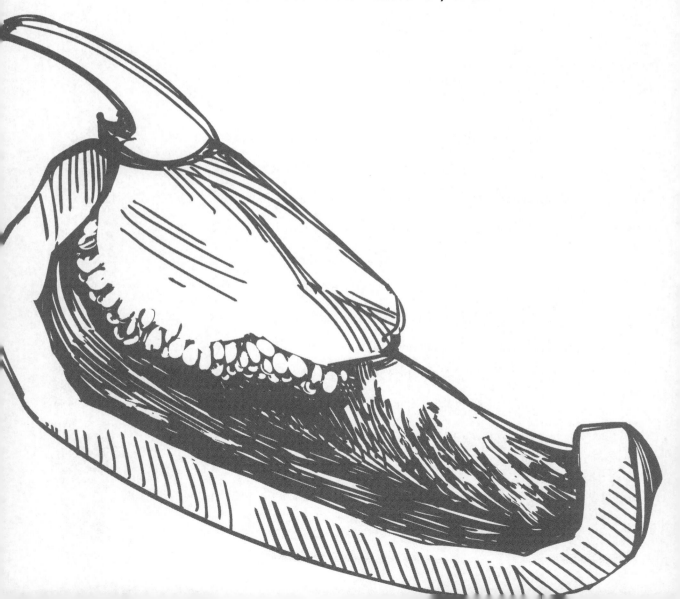

Classical
Spanish Beef Patties

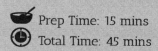
Prep Time: 15 mins
Total Time: 45 mins

Servings per Recipe: 8
Calories	522 kcal
Fat	34.7 g
Carbohydrates	36.7g
Protein	15.9 g
Cholesterol	40 mg
Sodium	505 mg

Ingredients

3 tbsps olive oil
1 lb ground beef
1 1/2 C. diced fresh cilantro
1 onion, diced
4 cloves garlic, minced

1 green bell pepper, diced
1 (8 oz.) can tomato sauce
1 (16 oz.) package egg roll wrappers
2 quarts vegetable oil for frying

Directions

1. Stir fry your bell pepper, onions, and garlic in olive oil until tender.
2. Combine in the meat and cook the meat until it is fully done.
3. Now add the cilantro and tomato sauce.
4. Heat the contents until the cilantro is soft then place everything to the side.
5. Now add 3 tbsps of the meat mix into an egg roll wrapper and shape the wrapper into a triangle.
6. Continue doing this until all your meat has been used up.
7. Now deep fry these patties in hot veggie oil until golden on both sides. Then place the patties on some paper towels before serving.
8. Enjoy.

PASTELON
(Beef Pie from Puerto Rico)

Prep Time: 25 mins
Total Time: 1 hr 10 mins

Servings per Recipe: 8

Calories	439 kcal
Fat	14.4 g
Carbohydrates	63.8g
Protein	19.9 g
Cholesterol	221 mg
Sodium	1042 mg

Ingredients

1 onion, cut into chunks
1 green bell pepper, cut into chunks
1 bunch fresh parsley
1 bunch fresh cilantro
1 bunch recao, or culantro
3 cloves garlic
1 tbsp water, or as needed
1 lb ground beef
1 (1.41 oz.) package sazon seasoning
ground black pepper to taste

1 pinch adobo seasoning, or to taste
olive oil
8 ripe plantains, peeled and cut on the bias
4 eggs, beaten
2 (15 oz.) cans green beans, drained
4 eggs, beaten

Directions

1. Blend the following with a blender or food processor: water, onion, garlic, bell peppers, recao, parsley, and cilantro.
2. Place the contents in a bowl with a covering of plastic and put everything in the fridge.
3. Now set your oven to 350 degrees before doing anything else.
4. Stir fry your beef until fully done then add in 2 tbsps of sofrito, adobo, sazon, and pepper.
5. Pour out any extra oils and place the beef to the side.
6. Now begin to fry your plantains for 5 mins then place half of them into a casserole dish.
7. Top the plantains with four whisked eggs and layer the beef on top.
8. Add your green beans next. Then add the rest of the plantains.
9. Finally add four more whisked eggs and also some adobo spice.
10. Cook everything in the oven for 35 mins.
11. Enjoy.

Bistec
Encebollao (Steak and Onions)

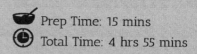

Prep Time: 15 mins
Total Time: 4 hrs 55 mins

Servings per Recipe: 6	
Calories	423 kcal
Fat	32.1 g
Carbohydrates	6.3g
Protein	26.4 g
Cholesterol	81 mg
Sodium	587 mg

Ingredients

2 lbs beef sirloin steak, sliced thinly across the grain
1/2 C. olive oil
2 tbsps minced garlic
1 pinch dried oregano
1 (.18 oz.) packet sazon seasoning

2 large white onions, sliced into rings
1/4 C. distilled white vinegar
1 C. beef stock
1 tsp salt

Directions

1. Get a bowl, combine: salt, steak, beef stock, olive oil, vinegar, garlic, onions, sazon, and oregano.
2. Place a covering of plastic over the dish after stirring the beef and place everything in the fridge for 5 hrs.
3. Add all of the mix into a large frying pan and get the mix boiling.
4. Once the mix is boiling, place a lid on the pan, set the heat to low, and cook everything for 45 mins.
5. Enjoy.

TOSTONES
(Spanish Plantains Fried)

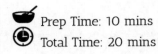

Prep Time: 10 mins
Total Time: 20 mins

Servings per Recipe: 2
Calories	136 kcal
Fat	3.3 g
Carbohydrates	28.5g
Protein	1.2 g
Cholesterol	0 mg
Sodium	14 mg

Ingredients

5 tbsps oil for frying
1 green plantain, peeled, diced into 1 inch pieces
3 C. cold water

salt to taste

Directions

1. Get your oil hot and begin to fry your plantains for 4 mins each side.
2. Place the plantains on a working surface and flatten them.
3. After all of your plantains have been flattened dip them in some water then fry the plantains again for 1 min per side.
4. Top them with salt after frying.
5. Enjoy.

Sofrito
(Latin Spice Mix)

Prep Time: 20 mins
Total Time: 20 mins

Servings per Recipe: 80
Calories	10 kcal
Fat	0.1 g
Carbohydrates	2.2g
Protein	0.4 g
Cholesterol	0 mg
Sodium	89 mg

Ingredients

2 green bell peppers, seeded and diced
1 red bell peppers, seeded and diced
10 ajies dulces peppers, tops removed
3 medium tomatoes, diced
4 onions, cut into large chunks
3 medium heads garlic, peeled

25 cilantro leaves with stems
25 leaves recao, or culantro
1 tbsp salt
1 tbsp black pepper

Directions

1. Blend the following with a blender: garlic, green peppers, onions, red peppers, tomatoes, red peppers, and ajies dulces.
2. Add in some black pepper, cilantro, salt, and the recao.
3. Continue blending until the mix resembles a salsa then place the contents in a sealable plastic container in the freezer.
4. Enjoy.
5. NOTE: To use the sofrito. Wait until the mix is frozen. Once it is frozen take the bag out of the freezer and scrape the ice with a tablespoon. Fill the tablespoon with the icy mix then add the scrapings into your dish as it cooks.
6. NOTE: Use this spice mix as a seasoning for anything you may be frying or stir frying in a pan. For example ground beef, or even rice.

CARNE
Guisada
(Latin Beef Stew)

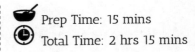
Prep Time: 15 mins
Total Time: 2 hrs 15 mins

Servings per Recipe: 4
Calories	677 kcal
Fat	46.5 g
Carbohydrates	18.5g
Protein	44.6 g
Cholesterol	155 mg
Sodium	971 mg

Ingredients

1 (8 oz.) can canned tomato sauce
1/4 C. sofrito sauce
1 (.18 oz.) packet sazon seasoning
1 tbsp adobo seasoning
1/2 tsp dried oregano
salt to taste

2 lbs beef stew meat
2 C. peeled, cubed potatoes
1 C. water

Directions

1. Get the following simmering in a saucepan: salt, tomato sauce, oregano, sofrito, adobo, and sazon.
2. Cook the mix for 7 mins then add in your meat and cook everything until it's fully done.
3. Add some water to submerge the meat then place a lid on the pot.
4. Cook everything for 60 mins then add in the potatoes and continue cooking the mix for 35 more mins.
5. Enjoy.

Habichuelas
Guisadas
(Latin Bean Stew)

🥘 Prep Time: 20 mins
🕐 Total Time: 20 mins

Servings per Recipe: 4
Calories   170 kcal
Fat   5.2 g
Carbohydrates   23.8g
Protein   8.3 g
Cholesterol   2 mg
Sodium   580 mg

Ingredients

1 tbsp olive oil
1/4 C. tomato sauce
2 tbsps sofrito sauce
1 (.18 oz.) packet sazon seasoning
1/4 tsp black pepper
2 C. cooked pinto beans, drained

1 1/2 C. water
salt to taste

Directions

1. For 5 mins heat and stir the following: pepper, oil, sazon, tomato sauce, and sofrito.
2. Combine in the salt, beans, and water.
3. Now turn up the heat to a medium level and cook everything for 20 mins.
4. Enjoy.

BUDIN
(Pudding in Puerto Rico)

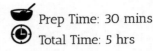

Prep Time: 30 mins
Total Time: 5 hrs

Servings per Recipe: 10
Calories   488 kcal
Fat   15.8 g
Carbohydrates   74.9 g
Protein   13.1 g
Cholesterol   116 mg
Sodium   656 mg

Ingredients

1 C. water
2 (3 inch) cinnamon sticks
15 whole cloves
1 tsp anise seed
2 tbsps water
1/2 C. white sugar
1 (1 lb) loaf day-old bread, crusts removed, cubed
4 C. evaporated milk

4 eggs
1 1/2 C. white sugar
1 tsp vanilla extract
3/4 tsp salt
1/4 C. butter, melted

Directions

1. Get 1 C. of water boiling then combine in the anise seeds, cinnamon sticks, and cloves.
2. Let this boil for 1 min then place a lid on the pot and shut the heat.
3. Let the contents stand on the stove for 20 mins.
4. At the same time stir and heat the following until the mix is smooth: 1/2 C. sugar and 2 tbsps water.
5. Once the mix begins to boil stop stirring and let the mix become a caramel color.
6. Once the sugar becomes a caramel color pour it into a bread pan and let it get hard.
7. Now set your oven to 350 degrees before doing anything else.
8. Add your bread cubes to a bowl and grab a sieve.
9. Pour the cinnamon water into the bowl through the sieve.
10. Now add the evaporated milk and stir the contents and let them sit for 12 mins.
11. Get a 2nd bowl, combine: melted butter, beaten eggs, salt, 1.5 C. sugar, and vanilla extract.
12. Combine both bowls then place the mix into the bread pan.
13. Now grab a roasting pan and place a towel in it. Then place the bread pan on top of the towel.

14. Add in some boiling water to the roasting pan to the halfway mark then place everything in the oven.
15. Cook the bread in the oven for 75 mins.
16. Now let the mix sit for 60 mins and then place it in the fridge for 3 hrs.
17. Place the pan on a serving dish upside down to invert the bread.
18. Enjoy.

PAELLA
I

🥘 Prep Time: 30 mins

🕐 Total Time: 1 hr

Servings per Recipe: 8
Calories	736 kcal
Fat	35.1 g
Carbohydrates	45.7g
Protein	55.7 g
Cholesterol	1202 mg
Sodium	1204 mg

Ingredients

2 tbsps olive oil
1 tbsp paprika
2 tsps dried oregano
salt and black pepper to taste
2 lbs skinless, boneless chicken breasts,
cut into 2 inch pieces
2 tbsps olive oil, divided
3 cloves garlic, crushed
1 tsp crushed red pepper flakes
2 C. uncooked short-grain white rice
1 pinch saffron threads
1 bay leaf
1/2 bunch Italian flat leaf parsley, diced

1 quart chicken stock
2 lemons, zested
2 tbsps olive oil
1 Spanish onion, diced
1 red bell pepper, coarsely diced
1 lb beef sausage, casings removed and
crumbled
1 lb shrimp, peeled and deveined

Directions

1. Get a bowl, combine: pepper, 1 tbsp olive oil, salt, paprika, and oregano.
2. Now add in your pieces of chicken and stir the meat to evenly coat it with the spice mix.
3. Place a covering of plastic around the bowl and put everything in the fridge.
4. Now in a big skillet add in 2 tbsp of olive oil.
5. Add in the rice, pepper flakes, and garlic.
6. Toast the contents for 4 mins then add: lemon zest, saffron, chicken stock, bay leaf, and parsley.
7. Get the mix boiling, place a lid on the pan, and cook the contents with a low heat for 22 mins.
8. At the same time begin to stir fry your onions and chicken in 2 tbsps of olive oil for 7 mins.

9. Now add in the sausage and bell pepper and cook them for 7 mins as well.
10. Now add the shrimp and cook them until they are done.
11. Top your rice with the meat mix and serve.
12. Enjoy.
13. NOTE: Paella is a truly authentic Latin Dish. It is also the cover image of this cookbook. The idea of Paella is to create an entire meal that fits in 1 big pan.

ASOPAO
de Pollo (Chicken and Rice Stew)

Prep Time: 25 mins
Total Time: 1 hr

Servings per Recipe: 6
Calories	550 kcal
Fat	17.7 g
Carbohydrates	55.2g
Protein	38.1 g
Cholesterol	131 mg
Sodium	2149 mg

Ingredients

2 lbs boneless, skinless chicken thighs
1/2 tsp ground black pepper
1 serving light adobo seasoning (such as Goya (R))
3 tbsps olive oil
1 green bell pepper, diced
1 red bell pepper, diced
1 medium onion, diced
4 cloves garlic, minced
2 tbsps tomato paste
1 1/2 C. medium-grain rice

2 (14.5 oz.) cans diced tomatoes
6 C. low-sodium chicken broth
1 bay leaf
1/4 tsp red pepper flakes, or to taste
1 C. frozen petite peas, thawed
1 C. sliced pimento-stuffed green olives
1/4 C. diced fresh cilantro

Directions

1. Coat your pieces of chicken with adobo and pepper.
2. Now begin to stir fry your tomato paste, green pepper, garlic, red pepper, and onions in hot oil for 5 mins. Now place everything to the side.
3. Sear your chicken for 6 mins per side then add back in the onion mix.
4. Also add in: pepper flakes, rice, bay leaf, broth, and diced tomatoes.
5. Get everything boiling then set the heat to a low level and cook the mix for 22 mins until the chicken is fully done and the rice is soft.
6. Now add the olives and peas.
7. Cook everything for 7 more mins then remove the bay leaf and add in some cilantro.
8. Enjoy.

Latin
Omelet

Prep Time: 15 mins
Total Time: 1 hr

Servings per Recipe: 6
Calories	252 kcal
Fat	21.5 g
Carbohydrates	10.7g
Protein	5.4 g
Cholesterol	124 mg
Sodium	54 mg

Ingredients

1/2 C. olive oil
1/2 lb potatoes, thinly sliced
salt and pepper to taste
1 large onion, thinly sliced
4 eggs
salt and pepper to taste

2 tomatoes - peeled, seeded, and coarsely diced
2 green onions, diced

Directions

1. Coat your potatoes with pepper and salt then fry them in olive oil until golden.
2. Now add in the onions and cook the mix for 7 mins until the onions are soft.
3. At the same time whisk your eggs with some pepper and salt then add the mix to the potatoes and onions.
4. Set the heat to low and continue cooking everything until the eggs become brown at the bottom.
5. Push a fork under the omelet to slightly loosen it then place a plate on top of the pan.
6. Now flip the pan. Then place the flipped omelet back in the pan.
7. Cook the omelet on its opposite side until the eggs become somewhat crispy.
8. Top everything with some green onions and tomatoes.
9. Enjoy.

CHICKEN
Fricassee I

🍳 Prep Time: 40 mins

🕐 Total Time: 6 hrs 40 mins

Servings per Recipe: 4

Calories	643 kcal
Fat	17.9 g
Carbohydrates	85.2g
Protein	32.7 g
Cholesterol	92 mg
Sodium	521 mg

Ingredients

1 lb chicken drumsticks, cleaned
1 tbsp adobo seasoning
1/2 (.18 oz.) packet sazon seasoning
1/2 tsp salt
5 large red potatoes, peeled and thickly sliced
1 large red bell pepper, seeded and diced
1 large green bell pepper, seeded and diced
1 large onion, diced

5 cloves garlic, minced
1 bunch fresh cilantro, diced
2 tbsps olive oil
1/2 C. broth
1 tsp ground cumin
1 tsp dried oregano
2 fresh or dried bay leaves

Directions

1. Coat your chicken with salt, sazon, and adobo.
2. Place them in the crock pot and slow cooker. Add the pieces of potato on top of the chicken.
3. Now begin to puree the following with a food processor: oregano, red pepper, cumin, green pepper, broth, onion, olive oil, garlic, and cilantro.
4. Add this mix to the slow cooker as well and also add in the bay leaves.
5. Place the lid on the crock pot and cook everything for 8 hrs with low heat.
6. Enjoy.

Restaurant Style
Clams I

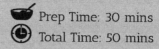

Prep Time: 30 mins
Total Time: 50 mins

Servings per Recipe: 6
Calories	697 kcal
Fat	52.6 g
Carbohydrates	9.1g
Protein	29.9 g
Cholesterol	104 mg
Sodium	1567 mg

Ingredients

5 lbs clams in shell, scrubbed clean,
remove any which are opened
1 1/2 lbs beef sausage, sliced into chunks
1 large onion, cut into thin wedges

1 (14.5 oz.) can diced tomatoes
2 C. broth
1/4 C. olive oil

Directions

1. Add the following to a big pot: clams, broth, sausage, tomatoes, and onions.
2. Place a lid on the pot and cook the mix with a high level of heat until your clams open.
3. When all the clams have opened add some olive oil and serve the dish in soup bowls with a liberal amount of broth.
4. Enjoy.

COUNTRYSIDE
Portuguese Potatoes

Prep Time: 30 mins
Total Time: 2 hrs

Servings per Recipe: 6

Calories	398 kcal
Fat	12 g
Carbohydrates	37.9 g
Protein	27.4 g
Cholesterol	65 mg
Sodium	279 mg

Ingredients

2 tbsps extra-virgin olive oil
1 lb beef stew meat, cut into cubes
1 tbsp all-purpose flour
8 cloves garlic, minced
2 bay leaves
1 pinch ground black pepper
1 pinch salt
1 onion, diced
1 green bell pepper, diced
1 carrot, diced
1 pinch paprika

1/2 fresh tomato, diced
1 C. broth
1 C. water
2 sprigs fresh parsley
3 red potatoes, peeled and cubed
1 sweet potato, peeled and cubed
1 (14.5 oz.) can green beans, drained

Directions

1. Coat your beef with flour and then add the following to a large pot with oil: pepper, beef, bay leaves, and garlic.
2. Once the beef is browned all over, about 7 mins of frying, add some salt.
3. Now add: paprika, onion, carrots, and green pepper.
4. Cook the onion mix for 7 mins. Then add: parsley, tomato, water, and broth.
5. Place a lid on the pot and cook everything for 35 mins.
6. Add the green beans and the sweet and red potatoes.
7. Let the potatoes cook for 50 mins.
8. Enjoy.

Fava Beans
Spanish Style

Prep Time: 15 mins

Total Time: 45 mins

Servings per Recipe: 8	
Calories	221 kcal
Fat	9.5 g
Carbohydrates	27.7g
Protein	7.4 g
Cholesterol	0 mg
Sodium	300 mg

Ingredients

5 tbsps olive oil
3 large onions, diced
2 cloves garlic, minced
2 tbsps red pepper flakes
1/4 C. tomato sauce
2 C. hot water

3 tbsps diced fresh parsley
salt to taste
1/2 tsp black pepper
2 tsps paprika
2 (19 oz.) cans fava beans

Directions

1. Stir fry your garlic and onions in oil until browned.
2. Now add paprika, pepper flakes, pepper, tomato sauce, salt, parsley, and hot water.
3. Get the mix boiling, set the heat to low, and cook everything for 35 mins.
4. Now add in your beans and shut the heat.
5. Let the beans sit in the mix for 15 mins with a lid on the pot.
6. Enjoy.

RICE
Casserole

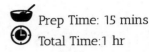 Prep Time: 15 mins
Total Time:1 hr

Servings per Recipe: 6

Calories	442 kcal
Fat	22.5 g
Carbohydrates	42g
Protein	17.4 g
Cholesterol	68 mg
Sodium	318 mg

Ingredients

3 C. water
1 1/2 C. uncooked white rice
1 tbsp butter
1 tbsp olive oil
1 tbsp olive oil
1 small onion, diced
2 cloves garlic, minced
2 (5 oz.) cans tuna, drained
3/4 C. heavy cream

3 tbsps ketchup
1 tsp hot pepper sauce
salt and pepper to taste
1/2 C. sliced black olives
1/2 C. shredded Cheddar cheese

Directions

1. Get the following boiling: 1 tbsp of olive oil, rice, butter, and water.
2. Once the mix is boiling, place a lid on the pot, and set the heat to a low level. Cook the rice for 27 mins.
3. Now set your oven to 350 degrees before doing anything else.
4. Stir fry your onions and garlic in 1 tbsp of olive oil for 7 mins then add the following: pepper, tuna, salt, hot sauce, ketchup, and cream.
5. Cook the contents for 12 mins.
6. Now add half of your rice to a casserole dish then top it with the tuna then add the rest of the rice.
7. Coat the layers with cheese and olives.
8. Cook the casserole in the oven for 25 mins.
9. Enjoy.

Cacoila
(Portuguese Beef)

Prep Time: 30 mins
Total Time: 14 hrs

Servings per Recipe: 6
Calories   437 kcal
Fat   30 g
Carbohydrates   10.8g
Protein   28.5 g
Cholesterol   101 mg
Sodium   91 mg

Ingredients

2 lbs beef stew meat, cleaned, cut into 1 inch cubes
3 oranges, juiced
1/4 C. broth
1 tsp hot pepper sauce
1 tsp vegetable oil

2 bay leaves
2 cloves garlic, crushed
1 tsp paprika
1/4 tsp ground allspice
salt and ground black pepper to taste

Directions

1. Get a bowl, add the following: pepper, pepper sauce, garlic, salt, orange juice, allspice, oil, paprika, bay leaves, and broth.
2. Place a covering on the bowl and put it all in the fridge for 8 hrs.
3. Now cook your beef and the sauce for 65 mins in a large pot.
4. Enjoy.

CHICKEN SOUP
from Spain

Prep Time: 10 mins
Total Time: 1 hr 10 mins

Servings per Recipe: 4
Calories   159 kcal
Fat   7.1 g
Carbohydrates   6.8g
Protein   16.8 g
Cholesterol   49 mg
Sodium   63 mg

Ingredients

1 whole bone-in chicken breast, with skin
1 onion, cut into thin wedges
4 sprigs fresh parsley
1/2 tsp lemon zest
1 sprig fresh mint
6 C. chicken stock

1/3 C. thin egg noodles
2 tbsps diced fresh mint leaves
salt to taste
1/4 tsp freshly ground white pepper

Directions

1. Gently boil the following for 40 mins: mint sprig, chicken breast, lemon zest, parsley, and onions.
2. Take out the chicken and cut it into strips.
3. Now run the broth through a strainer and add it back to the pot.
4. Get the broth boiling, then add the diced mint and the pasta.
5. Add some white pepper and salt as well.
6. Cook the pasta for about 9 mins then shut the heat and add in: chicken and lemon juice.
7. Divide the soup amongst your serving dishes and garnish each one with mint and a piece of lemon.
8. Enjoy.

Spanish
Clams

Prep Time: 10 mins
Total Time: 30 mins

Servings per Recipe: 4
Calories	435 kcal
Fat	30.5 g
Carbohydrates	23.2g
Protein	12.9 g
Cholesterol	46 mg
Sodium	910 mg

Ingredients

24 small clams in shell, scrubbed
1/4 C. cornmeal
1/4 C. olive oil
3 cloves garlic, minced
8 oz. beef sausage, diced
1 medium red onion, sliced
1 pinch red pepper flakes (optional)

1 (12 fluid oz.) chicken broth
1 (8 oz.) bottle clam juice
1 (28 oz.) can crushed roma tomatoes
3 tbsps diced fresh oregano
1 pinch salt and pepper to taste

Directions

1. Submerge your clams in water, in a saucepan, then add the cornmeal.
2. Let the contents sit for 25 mins then run the clams until water.
3. Stir fry your garlic in olive oil for 5 mins then add: red pepper flakes, chourico, and onions.
4. Cook the mix for 4 mins. Then add your broth and let the mix cook for 5 mins.
5. Now add in the clams, tomatoes, and clam juice.
6. Place a lid on the pan and cook the contents until the clams open.
7. Add pepper, salt, and oregano.
8. Enjoy.

PORTUGUESE
Green Soup (Caldo Verde)

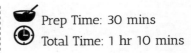

Prep Time: 30 mins
Total Time: 1 hr 10 mins

Servings per Recipe: 6
Calories   456 kcal
Fat   27 g
Carbohydrates   44.7g
Protein   11 g
Cholesterol   26 mg
Sodium   1144 mg

Ingredients

3 tbsps olive oil
1 onion, finely diced
3 cloves garlic, crushed
6 potatoes, peeled and thinly sliced
1 lb cabbage, thinly sliced
2 quarts water
8 oz. beef sausage, casing removed,

sliced 1/4-inch thick
1 tsp smoked paprika
2 tsps salt
pepper to taste
olive oil

Directions

1. Stir fry your garlic and onions in 3 tbsps of olive oil for 5 mins then add half of your cabbage and the potatoes.
2. Cook the cabbage for 5 mins.
3. Add the water and get everything boiling.
4. Place a lid on the pot and let the contents gently boil over medium heat for 17 mins.
5. Now with an immersion blender puree the soup.
6. Then get everything hot again.
7. Add in the rest of the cabbage, the sausage, some pepper, salt, and paprika.
8. Get the mix simmering and then place the lid back on the pot.
9. Cook the contents for 7 mins.
10. Divide the soup between your serving bowls and top everything with some olive oil
11. Enjoy.

Restaurant Style
Rabbit

Prep Time: 15 mins
Total Time: 1 hr 15 mins

Servings per Recipe: 4

Calories	570 kcal
Fat	29.7 g
Carbohydrates	13.8g
Protein	48.9 g
Cholesterol	139 mg
Sodium	347 mg

Ingredients

1 (2 lb) rabbit, cleaned and cut into pieces
salt and pepper to taste
3 tbsps prepared mustard
3 tbsps vegetable oil
1 C. broth

4 small onions
2 slices turkey bacon, cut into 1/2 inch pieces
1 orange

Directions

1. Set your oven to 350 degrees before doing anything else.
2. Coat your rabbit with some pepper and salt. Then top it evenly with mustard.
3. Combine the seasoned meat, in a Dutch oven, with broth and oil.
4. Then add the onions and the bacon.
5. Cook the contents in the oven for 35 mins with the lid on the pot then flip the meat and add some squeezed orange juice.
6. Cook everything for 35 more mins without the lid.
7. Enjoy with cooked mashed potato.

SOUTH AMERICAN
Banana Pie

Prep Time: 20 mins
Total Time: 1 hr 5 mins

Servings per Recipe: 12
Calories   451 kcal
Fat   11.2 g
Carbohydrates   82.5g
Protein   11.1 g
Cholesterol   0 mg
Sodium   126 mg

Ingredients

3 tbsps brown sugar
1/2 C. water
10 bananas, peeled and sliced
lengthwise
2 C. whole wheat flour
2 C. toasted wheat germ
3 C. rolled oats

1 C. packed brown sugar
1 C. light margarine
1 tbsp cinnamon

Directions

1. Set your oven to 350 degrees before doing anything else.
2. In a saucepan add in 3 tbsps of brown sugar and heat it until it melts. Then add some water and stir everything until the sugar and water are completely combined.
3. Add this syrup to a pie dish and cover the bottom. Now layer a covering of bananas.
4. Get a bowl, combine: 1 C. brown sugar, margarine, wheat flour, oats, and wheat germ.
5. Now with your hands make a dough that is somewhat crumbly.
6. Add 1/2 of this mix over the bananas then add the rest of the bananas and top them with cinnamon.
7. Press everything down and add the rest of the dough.
8. Cook the contents in the oven for 50 mins.
9. Enjoy.

Spanish Greens

🥄 Prep Time: 10 mins
🕐 Total Time: 2 hrs 10 mins

Servings per Recipe: 6
Calories	269 kcal
Fat	19.4 g
Carbohydrates	10.1g
Protein	15.1 g
Cholesterol	32 mg
Sodium	744 mg

Ingredients

1/2 lb peppered turkey bacon, diced
1 onion, diced
2 lbs collard greens - rinsed, stemmed and torn into 3x6 inch pieces
1 C. chicken stock

1 tsp cayenne pepper
2 tbsps apple cider vinegar

Directions

1. Stir fry your bacon until fully done then add the onions and cook them for 6 mins. Add the greens then add the stock and cayenne.
2. Get the mix boiling and set the heat to low.
3. Cook everything for 80 mins.
4. Now add in the apple cider vinegar and cook for 17 more mins until half of the juices have evaporated.
5. Enjoy.

A LEMONADE
From Brazil

Prep Time: 10 mins
Total Time: 10 mins

Servings per Recipe: 4
Calories   152 kcal
Fat   1.3 g
Cholesterol   36.2g
Sodium   1.4 g
Carbohydrates   5 mg
Protein   28 mg

Ingredients

2 limes
1/2 C. sugar
3 tbsp sweetened condensed milk
3 C. water

ice

Directions

1. Cut off the ends and slice the each lime into eight wedges.
2. In a blender, add the sugar, sweetened condensed milk, water and ice and pulse for about 5 times.
3. Through a mesh strainer, strain to remove the rinds.
4. Serve over the ice.

Rio De Janeiro Style
Collard Greens

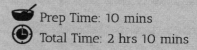 Prep Time: 10 mins

Total Time: 2 hrs 10 mins

Servings per Recipe: 6

Calories	269 kcal
Fat	19.4 g
Carbohydrates	10.1g
Protein	15.1 g
Cholesterol	32 mg
Sodium	744 mg

Ingredients

1/2 lb. peppered turkey bacon, diced
1 onion, chopped
2 lb. collard greens - rinsed, stemmed and
torn into 3x6 inch pieces
1 C. chicken stock

1 tsp cayenne pepper
2 tbsp apple cider vinegar

Directions

1. Heat a heavy-bottomed pan on medium-high heat and cook the bacon till browned.
2. Discard most of the bacon grease from the pan.
3. Add the onion and cook for about 4 minutes.
4. Stir in the collard greens and add the broth and cayenne pepper.
5. Reduce the heat to low and cook for about 75 minutes.
6. Stir in the apple cider vinegar and cook for about 15 minutes.

CINNAMON
Brazilian
Pineapple

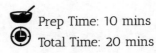
Prep Time: 10 mins
Total Time: 20 mins

Servings per Recipe: 6
Calories   255 kcal
Fat   0.3 g
Carbohydrates   66.4g
Protein   1.3 g
Cholesterol   0 mg
Sodium   13 mg

Ingredients

1 C. brown sugar
2 tsp ground cinnamon
1 pineapple - peeled, cored, and cut into
6 wedges

Directions

1. Set your outdoor grill for medium-high heat and lightly, grease the grill grate.
2. In a bowl, add the brown sugar and cinnamon and beat well.
3. Transfer the sugar mixture into a large resealable plastic bag.
4. Add the pineapple wedges and shake to coat evenly.
5. Cook the pineapple wedges on the grill for about 3-5 minutes from both sides.

Brazilian
Fudge

Prep Time: 10 mins
Total Time: 25 mins

Servings per Recipe: 12
Calories   306 kcal
Fat   14.7 g
Cholesterol   37.9 g
Sodium   8.3 g
Carbohydrates   11 mg
Protein   268 mg

Ingredients

1 (8 oz.) jar roasted peanuts, skins removed
1 (8 oz.) package tea biscuits (such as Marie Biscuits)
2 tbsp white sugar

1 (14 oz.) can sweetened condensed milk

Directions

1. Line a 9-inch square baking dish with a wax paper.
2. In a food processor, add the peanuts and biscuits and pulse till the mixture resembles coarse flour.
3. Add the sugar and pulse till well combined.
4. Add the sweetened condensed milk and pulse till the mixture forms a ball that pulls away from the sides of the food processor bowl.
5. Transfer the mixture into the prepared dish and with your hands, press into an even layer.
6. Keep aside for at least 15 minutes or up to overnight.
7. Remove from the dish and cut into squares to serve.
8. Store in air-tight containers between uses.

3-INGREDIENT
Beef Ribs Brazilian

Prep Time: 10 mins
Total Time: 6 hrs 20 mins

Servings per Recipe: 3
Calories	698 kcal
Fat	56.5 g
Carbohydrates	0g
Protein	44.1 g
Cholesterol	163 mg
Sodium	3647 mg

Ingredients

1 (3 lb.) rack of whole beef ribs (not short ribs)
2 tbsp sea salt, or more if needed
3/4 C. water

Directions

1. Set your oven to 275 degrees F before doing anything else.
2. Place the rack of beef ribs on a work surface with the shiny white membrane facing up.
3. Slip the blade of a sharp knife under the membrane at one end, and slice the membrane off the meat in a single piece.
4. Discard the chewy membrane and rub the ribs with the salt evenly.
5. Arrange the ribs onto a cooking rack in a roasting pan.
6. Cook in the oven for about 1 1/2 hours.
7. Lightly baste the beef with the water.
8. Cook for 4 1/2 hours more, Basting after every 45 minutes.
9. Remove from the oven and keep aside to cool for about 10-15 minutes before slicing.

Classical
Brazilian Banana Bread

Prep Time: 25 mins
Total Time: 1 hr

Servings per Recipe: 12

Calories	355 kcal
Fat	4.7 g
Carbohydrates	74.3g
Protein	6.1 g
Cholesterol	53 mg
Sodium	140 mg

Ingredients

3 tbsp margarine
2 C. white sugar
3 egg yolks
3 C. all-purpose flour
1 tbsp baking powder
1 C. milk
3 egg whites

6 bananas, peeled and sliced
2 tbsp white sugar
1 tsp ground cinnamon

Directions

1. Set your oven to 350 degrees F before doing anything else and grease and flour a 13x9-inch pan.
2. In a large bowl, add the margarine and sugar and beat till smooth.
3. Add the yolks and beat till well combined.
4. Slowly, add the flour and baking powder alternately with the milk, mix till well combined.
5. In another bowl, add the egg whites and beat till doubled in the volume.
6. Fold the beaten whites into the dough.
7. Transfer the mixture into the prepared pan.
8. Arrange the banana slices over the top of the dough evenly.
9. In a small bowl, mix together the 2 tbsp of the sugar and the cinnamon and sprinkle over the banana slices.
10. Cook in the oven for about 30-35 minutes or until a toothpick inserted into the center comes out clean.

CLASSICAL
Brazilian Banana Pie

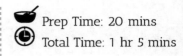

Prep Time: 20 mins
Total Time: 1 hr 5 mins

Servings per Recipe: 12
Calories	451 kcal
Fat	11.2 g
Carbohydrates	82.5g
Protein	11.1 g
Cholesterol	0 mg
Sodium	126 mg

Ingredients

3 tbsp brown sugar
1/2 C. water
10 bananas, peeled and sliced lengthwise
2 C. whole wheat flour
2 C. toasted wheat germ
3 C. rolled oats

1 C. packed brown sugar
1 C. light margarine
1 tbsp cinnamon

Directions

1. Set your oven to 350 degrees F before doing anything else.
2. In a small pan, add 3 tbsp of the brown sugar on medium heat and cook till melted.
3. Add the water and stir till the sugar is completely dissolved.
4. Heat the mixture between 234 and 240 degrees F.
5. In the bottom of a deep pie dish, place the syrup and tilt the dish to coat the bottom.
6. Place a layer of the bananas on top of the melted sugar.
7. In a medium bowl, mix together the whole wheat flour, wheat germ, oats and 1 C. of the brown sugar.
8. Add the margarine and with your hands, pinch it into small pieces to make a crumbly mixture.
9. Sprinkle half of the crumbly mixture over the bananas in the dish and gently, pat down.
10. Top with the remaining bananas and sprinkle with about half of the cinnamon.
11. Spread the remaining crumbly mixture over the bananas and gently, pat the pie smoothly
12. Sprinkle the remaining cinnamon over the top.
13. Cook in the oven for about 45 minutes or till a toothpick inserted into the center comes out clean.

Carrot
Cake

🥣 Prep Time: 20 mins
🕐 Total Time: 1 hr

Servings per Recipe: 12
Calories	529 kcal
Fat	22.7 g
Carbohydrates	77.7g
Protein	5.7 g
Cholesterol	68 mg
Sodium	232 mg

Ingredients

3 large carrots, peeled and thinly sliced
4 eggs
1 C. cooking oil
2 C. white sugar
2 C. all-purpose flour
1 tbsp baking powder
2 tbsp butter or margarine

1 C. white sugar
1 C. instant hot chocolate mix
3/4 C. milk

Directions

1. Set your oven to 350 degrees F before doing anything else and lightly, grease 13x9-inch baking dish.
2. In a food processor, add the carrots, eggs, and oil and pulse till the carrots are chopped finely.
3. Transfer the carrot mixture into a bowl.
4. Add 2 C. of the sugar till well combined.
5. Add the flour and baking powder and mix till well combined.
6. Transfer the mixture into the prepared baking dish.
7. Cook in the oven for about 40 minutes.
8. Meanwhile for the icing in a pan, place the butter, 1 C. of the sugar, instant hot chocolate drink mix and milk on medium heat.
9. Heat, stirring to almost boiling and mixture becomes thick.
10. Remove the baking dish from the oven and immediately spread the icing over the top of the cake evenly.

PUDDING
Brazilian Style

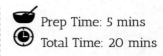 Prep Time: 5 mins

Total Time: 20 mins

Servings per Recipe: 10
Calories	163 kcal
Fat	5.4 g
Carbohydrates	24.2g
Protein	5.2 g
Cholesterol	69 mg
Sodium	87 mg

Ingredients

1 (14 oz.) can sweetened condensed milk
3 eggs
3 tbsp hot chocolate mix

3 tbsp shredded coconut

Directions

1. In a blender, add the sweetened condensed milk, eggs, hot chocolate mix and shredded coconut and pulse till smooth and creamy.
2. In a microwave-safe bowl, place the mixture and microwave on High for about 10 to 12 minutes.
3. Refrigerate to cool before serving.

Brazilian
Tilapia Fish Stew

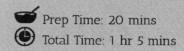

Prep Time: 20 mins
Total Time: 1 hr 5 mins

Servings per Recipe: 6

Calories	359 kcal
Fat	21.8 g
Carbohydrates	15.6g
Protein	27.4 g
Cholesterol	42 mg
Sodium	600 mg

Ingredients

3 tbsp lime juice
1 tbsp ground cumin
1 tbsp paprika
2 tsp minced garlic
1 tsp salt
1 tsp ground black pepper
1 1/2 lb. tilapia fillets, cut into chunks

2 tbsp olive oil
2 onions, chopped
4 large bell peppers, sliced
1 (16 oz.) can diced tomatoes, drained
1 (16 oz.) can coconut milk
1 bunch fresh cilantro, chopped

Directions

1. In a bowl, mix together the lime juice, cumin, paprika, garlic, salt and pepper.
2. Add the tilapia and toss to coat well.
3. Refrigerate, covered for at least 20 minutes up to 24 hours.
4. In a large pan, heat the oil on medium-high heat and sauté the onions for about 1-2 minutes.
5. Reduce the heat to medium and place the bell peppers, tilapia, and diced tomatoes in the pan in the succeeding layers.
6. Place the coconut milk over the mixture and simmer, covered for about 15 minutes, stirring occasionally.
7. Stir in the cilantro and simmer till the tilapia and simmer for about 5-10 minutes.

PAO
de Queijo (Authentic Cheese Rolls)

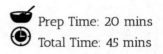

Prep Time: 20 mins
Total Time: 45 mins

Servings per Recipe: 14
Calories   199 kcal
Fat   12 g
Carbohydrates   17.2g
Protein   5.8 g
Cholesterol   36 mg
Sodium   386 mg

Ingredients

2 C. tapioca starch
1 tsp salt
1/2 C. vegetable oil
1/3 C. water
1/3 C. milk

2 eggs
6 oz. shredded Parmesan cheese

Directions

1. Set your oven to 375 degrees F before doing anything else and lightly, grease a baking sheet.
2. In a large bowl, add the tapioca starch and salt.
3. In a pan, add the vegetable oil, water and milk and bring to a boil on medium heat till a white foam appears.
4. Place the milk mixture over the tapioca starch and stir till well combined and keep aside for about 15 minutes.
5. Add the eggs and Parmesan cheese and mix till well combined.
6. Make about 1 1/2-inch balls from the dough and arrange on the prepared baking sheet.
7. Cook in the oven for about 15-20 minutes.

South American
Turkey

🥣 Prep Time: 25 mins
🕐 Total Time: 3 hrs 45 mins

Servings per Recipe: 12
Calories	662 kcal
Fat	33.3 g
Cholesterol	7.9g
Sodium	79.3 g
Carbohydrates	224 mg
Protein	504 mg

Ingredients

10 large Roma tomatoes, halved and seeded
1 large green bell pepper, halved and seeded
2 tbsp vegetable oil
1 (10 lb.) whole turkey, neck and giblets removed
1 Granny Smith apple - peeled, quartered, and cored
1 (5 oz.) jar pitted green olives, drained
2 dried ancho chilis, stemmed and seeded

1/2 C. raw pumpkin seeds
2 bay leaves
1 onion, cut into chunks
salt and pepper to taste

Directions

1. Set the broiler of your oven and arrange oven rack in the topmost position.
2. Line a baking sheet with a piece of the foil.
3. Arrange the tomatoes and bell pepper onto the prepared baking sheet, cut-side down.
4. Cook under the broiler for about 5 minutes.
5. Place charred vegetables into a bowl and immediately with a plastic wrap, seal tightly till the skins loosen.
6. Now, set your oven to 325 degrees F.
7. Meanwhile in a large roasting pan, heat the vegetable oil on medium-high heat and sear the turkey till browned from all the sides.
8. Remove from the heat and arrange the turkey, breast side up in the roasting pan.
9. Stuff the turkey cavity with the quartered apples and olives.
10. Heat a skillet on medium-high heat and sauté the ancho chilis, pumpkin seeds and bay leaves for about 5 minutes.

11. Remove from the heat and keep aside to cool slightly.
12. Remove the skin of the tomatoes and peppers.
13. In a blender, add the ancho chilis mixture, tomatoes, green peppers, onion, salt and pepper and pulse till a thick and smooth sauce is formed.
14. Coat the turkey with the sauce evenly.
15. Cook in the oven for about 3 hours, basting with the pan juices occasionally.

Platanos
Maduros

Prep Time: 5 mins
Total Time: 15 mins

Servings per Recipe: 4
Calories   323 kcal
Fat   14.1 g
Cholesterol   51g
Sodium   1.8 g
Carbohydrates   0 mg
Protein   6 mg

Ingredients

2 large very ripe (black) plantains - peeled
1/4 C. vegetable oil
1 tbsp vanilla extract

1 tsp ground cinnamon
2 tbsp white sugar, or to taste (optional)

Directions

1. Cut each plantain into 2 halves and then each half into 3 strips.
2. In a large skillet, heat the vegetable oil on medium-high heat.
3. Gently, place the plantain strips in the skillet evenly.
4. Drizzle with the vanilla extract and sprinkle with the cinnamon.
5. Cook, covered for about 5-7 minutes per side.
6. Transfer the plantains onto a paper towel lined plate to drain.
7. Serve with a sprinkling of the sugar.

TRADITIONAL
Honduran Holiday Cake

Prep Time: 25 mins
Total Time: 2 hrs 10 min

Servings per Recipe: 16

Calories	515 kcal
Fat	23.4 g
Cholesterol	68g
Sodium	9.9 g
Carbohydrates	73 mg
Protein	478 mg

Ingredients

1 1/2 C. margarine
3 C. white sugar
2 C. sifted all-purpose flour
1 C. rice flour
1 tbsp baking powder
6 room-temperature eggs
2 C. lukewarm milk

2 C. grated Parmesan cheese
1/2 C. white sugar
1/4 C. all-purpose flour
1/4 C. sesame seeds

Directions

1. Set your oven to 350 degrees F before doing anything else and lightly, grease and flour a medium glass baking dish.
2. In a bowl, add the margarine and 3 C. of the sugar and beat till fluffy.
3. Add the eggs, one at a time and mix well.
4. In another bowl, mix together 2 C of the all-purpose flour, rice flour and baking powder.
5. Add the flour mixture alternating with the milk and mix till well combined.
6. Slowly, stir in the Parmesan cheese.
7. In a small bowl, mix together 1/2 C. of the sugar, 1/4 C. of the all-purpose flour and sesame seeds.
8. Transfer the flour mixture into the prepared baking dish evenly and sprinkle with the sesame seeds mixture.
9. Cook in the oven for about 45 minutes or till a toothpick inserted in the center comes out clean.
10. Remove from the oven and keep onto a wire rack to cool completely.
11. Cut into desired sized squares and serve.

Avocado
and Fried Bean Tacos from Honduras (Baleadas)

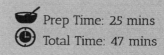 Prep Time: 25 mins

Total Time: 47 mins

Servings per Recipe: 8
Calories   390 kcal
Fat   23.1 g
Cholesterol   36.9 g
Sodium   10.1 g
Carbohydrates   43 mg
Protein   368 mg

Ingredients

Tortillas:
2 C. all-purpose flour
1 C. water
1/2 C. vegetable oil
1 egg
1/2 tsp salt
Filling:

2 C. refried beans, warmed
1 avocado, sliced
1/2 C. crumbled queso fresco
1/4 C. crema fresca

Directions

1. In a large bowl, add the flour, water, vegetable oil, egg and salt and mix till a smooth dough is formed.
2. Make 8 golf ball-sized balls from the dough.
3. Cover the balls and keep aside for about 20 minutes.
4. Stretch each dough ball into a thick tortilla.
5. Heat a large skillet on medium-high heat and cook each tortilla for about 1 minute per side.
6. Place the refried beans, avocado and queso fresco over each tortilla evenly and drizzle with the crema.
7. Fold each tortilla in half over the filling.

TACOS
from Honduras with Chicken Tomato Sauce

Prep Time: 25 mins
Total Time: 1 hr 11 mins

Servings per Recipe: 5
Calories	347 kcal
Fat	11 g
Cholesterol	49.4g
Sodium	15.6 g
Carbohydrates	23 mg
Protein	694 mg

Ingredients

2 skinless, boneless chicken breasts
1/2 tsp salt
1 tbsp vegetable oil
1 onion, finely chopped
1 tomato, finely chopped
1 green bell pepper, finely chopped
1 tsp chicken bouillon granules
1/2 tsp ground black pepper
1 lb corn tortillas
vegetable oil for frying

Tomato Sauce:
1/4 C. water
1 (6.5 oz.) can tomato sauce
1/2 tsp chicken bouillon granules
1/2 tsp seasoned salt

Directions

1. In a pan, add the chicken breasts, salt in a pot and enough water to cover halfway and bring to a boil.
2. Cook for about 15 minutes.
3. Remove from the heat and keep aside to cool for about 5 minutes.
4. Shred the chicken breasts into thin pieces.
5. In a large skillet, heat 1 tbsp of the vegetable oil on medium heat and cook the onion, tomato and green bell peppers for about 2 minutes.
6. Stir in the shredded chicken, 1 tsp of the chicken bouillon and black pepper and cook for about 5 minutes.
7. Place some of the chicken mixture in the middle of each corn tortilla.
8. Fold each tortilla around the filling and secure with a toothpick.
9. In a large pan, heat the oil to 350 degrees F and fry the tortillas in batches for about 2 minutes per side.
10. Transfer the tortillas onto a paper towel lined plate to drain.

11. In a small pan, add 1/4 C. of the water and bring to a boil.

12. Add the tomato sauce, 1/2 tsp of the chicken bouillon and seasoned salt on medium-high heat and cook for about 5 minutes.

13. Place the sauce over the tacos and serve.

5-INGREDIENT
Costa Rican Potato Salad

Prep Time: 20 mins
Total Time: 2 hrs 10 min

Servings per Recipe: 6

Calories	212 kcal
Fat	7.2 g
Cholesterol	30.3g
Sodium	7.7 g
Carbohydrates	126 mg
Protein	219 mg

Ingredients

4 potatoes, peeled and cubed
1 (15 oz.) can sliced beets, drained and finely chopped
4 eggs

2 tbsp mayonnaise
salt and pepper to taste

Directions

1. In a pan of the salted water, add the potatoes on high heat and bring to a boil.
2. Reduce the heat to medium-low and simmer, covered for about 20 minutes.
3. Drain well and let the potatoes steam dry for about 1-2 minutes.
4. Keep aside to cool completely.
5. Meanwhile in a pan, add the eggs in a single layer and enough water to cover on high heat.
6. Cover the pan and bring to a boil.
7. Remove from the heat and keep aside, covered for about 15 minutes.
8. Drain the eggs and rinse under running cold water to cool.
9. After cooling, peel and chop the eggs.
10. In a bowl, add the potatoes, beets, eggs, mayonnaise, salt and pepper and mix well.

Costa Rican
Dinner (Ground Beef and Plantains) (Easy Picadillo)

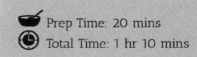 Prep Time: 20 mins
Total Time: 1 hr 10 mins

Servings per Recipe: 8

Calories	203 kcal
Fat	7.9 g
Cholesterol	29.8g
Sodium	6.1 g
Carbohydrates	24 mg
Protein	623 mg

Ingredients

4 plantains, peeled and cut into 3 pieces
1/2 lb. ground beef
2 cloves garlic, minced
2 tbsp minced onion
2 tsp salt
1/2 tsp pepper
1 1/2 tbsp chopped cilantro

1/2 C. tomato, chopped
2 tsp Worcestershire sauce
1 dash hot pepper sauce

Directions

1. In a pan of the salted water, add the plantains on medium-high heat and cook till tender.
2. Drain well and keep aside to cool.
3. After cooling, chop the plantains finely.
4. In a large skillet, heat the oil on medium-high heat and cook the beef, garlic, and onion, salt and pepper till the beef is browned.
5. Stir in the chopped plantain, cilantro, tomato, Worcestershire sauce and hot pepper sauce and cook for about 10 minutes.

SWEET
Papaya Milk (Batido)

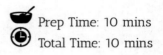

Prep Time: 10 mins
Total Time: 10 mins

Servings per Recipe: 6
Calories   128 kcal
Fat   4.8 g
Cholesterol   17.2g
Sodium   4.4 g
Carbohydrates   18 mg
Protein   69 mg

Ingredients

1 (12 fluid oz.) can evaporated milk
1 C. chopped papaya
1/4 C. white sugar
1 tsp vanilla extract

1 pinch ground cinnamon
1 tray ice cubes

Directions

1. In a blender, add the milk, papaya, sugar, vanilla extract and cinnamon and pulse till smooth.
2. Add the ice and pulse till slushy.

Central American
Gingerbread from Panama

Prep Time: 20 mins
Total Time: 3 hrs 15 mins

Servings per Recipe: 70
Calories   127 kcal
Fat   1.6 g
Cholesterol   26.9 g
Sodium   1.4 g
Carbohydrates   0 mg
Protein   29 mg

Ingredients

7 1/4 C. all-purpose flour
1/2 tsp salt
1/2 tsp baking powder
1/2 C. vegetable shortening

3/4 lb. fresh ginger root, minced
2 pints molasses

Directions

1. Set your oven to 350 degrees F before doing anything else and grease and flour a 15x20-inch baking dish.
2. In a bowl, mix together the flour, salt and baking powder.
3. In another large bowl, add the shortening, ginger and molasses and mix till smooth.
4. Add the flour mixture and mix till smooth.
5. Place the mixture into the prepared baking dish evenly.
6. Cook in the oven for about 40-45 minutes or till a toothpick inserted in the center comes out clean.
7. Remove from the oven and keep on wire rack to cool for about 15 minutes.
8. Cut into 2-inch squares and keep aside to cool for about 2-3 hours before serving.

FULL
Latin Dinner (Chicken and Rice)

Prep Time: 15 mins
Total Time: 2 hrs 10 mir

Servings per Recipe: 8
Calories   535 kcal
Fat   20.2 g
Cholesterol   36.3g
Sodium   50.5 g
Carbohydrates   142 mg
Protein   1105 mg

Ingredients

1/4 C. vegetable oil
1 (4 to 6 lb.) whole chicken, cut into pieces
1 onion, chopped
1 green bell pepper, chopped
2 cloves garlic, minced
2 cloves garlic
1 (14.5 oz.) can stewed tomatoes
1 C. rice
2 tsp salt

1 tsp dried oregano
1/2 tsp ground black pepper
1 bay leaf
2 C. chicken stock
1 C. green peas
1/2 C. sliced black olives
1/2 C. raisins
1/4 C. chopped pimento peppers

Directions

1. Set your oven to 350 degrees F before doing anything else.
2. In a Dutch oven, heat the vegetable oil on medium heat and sear the chicken pieces for about 5-10 minutes.
3. With a slotted spoon, transfer the chicken pieces onto a plate.
4. In the same pan, add the onion, green bell pepper, minced garlic and whole garlic cloves and sauté for about 5 minutes.
5. Add the cooked chicken pieces, tomatoes, rice, salt, oregano, black pepper, bay leaf and enough chicken stock to cover the mixture.
6. Transfer the pan into the oven and cook for about 1 1/2 hours.
7. Stir in the peas, olives, raisins and pimento peppers and cook in the oven for about 15 minutes.

South American
Sweet Oat Drink
(Bebida de Avena)

Prep Time: 10 mins
Total Time: 1 hr 15 mins

Servings per Recipe: 5

Calories	329 kcal
Fat	7.9 g
Cholesterol	54.4g
Sodium	8.3 g
Carbohydrates	27 mg
Protein	112 mg

Ingredients

6 C. water
1 C. rolled oats
2 C. cold water
1 (14 oz.) can sweetened condensed milk

2 tbsp vanilla extract
1 pinch ground cinnamon

Directions

1. In a tall pan, add the water and bring to a boil.
2. Add the oats and cook for about 5 minutes, stirring occasionally.
3. Remove from the heat and stir in the cold water, condensed milk and vanilla extract.
4. Transfer the oat mixture into a pitcher and refrigerate to chill for at least 1 hour.
5. Transfer the drink into the serving glasses and serve with a sprinkling of the cinnamon.

EASTER
Cinnamon Meringue

Prep Time: 15 mins
Total Time: 30 mins

Servings per Recipe: 8
Calories	142 kcal
Fat	4.3 g
Cholesterol	25.6g
Sodium	0.7 g
Carbohydrates	26 mg
Protein	58 mg

Ingredients

4 C. tapioca starch
3/4 C. white sugar
1/2 C. butter, softened
2 eggs, beaten

1/2 tsp ground cinnamon
1/4 tsp salt

Directions

1. Set your oven to 350 degrees F before doing anything else and line 2 baking sheets with the parchment papers.
2. In a large bowl, add the tapioca flour, sugar, butter, eggs, cinnamon and salt and mix till a soft dough is formed.
3. Pinch off a small piece of the dough and roll onto a smooth surface into a pencil sized rope.
4. Coil the rope tightly into a spiral.
5. Repeat with the remaining dough.
6. Arrange the spirals onto the prepared baking sheets.
7. Cook in the oven for about 15 minutes.

Authentic
Colombian Hot Sauce

Prep Time: 10 mins
Total Time: 10 mins

Servings per Recipe: 16
Calories	7 kcal
Fat	< 0.1 g
Cholesterol	< 1.7g
Sodium	< 0.4 g
Carbohydrates	< 0 mg
Protein	294 mg

Ingredients

10 jalapeno peppers, seeded
1/4 C. water
1/4 C. white vinegar
1/4 C. fresh lemon juice

1 1/2 C. chopped green onions
1 C. chopped cilantro
2 tsp salt

Directions

1. In a blender, add all the ingredients and pulse till smooth.

2. Refrigerate before serving.

LENTILS
in Bogota

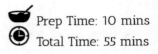
Prep Time: 10 mins
Total Time: 55 mins

Servings per Recipe: 3
Calories   201 kcal
Fat   5.3 g
Cholesterol   31.1g
Sodium   9.3 g
Carbohydrates   0 mg
Protein   789 mg

Ingredients

1/2 C. lentils
1 1/2 C. water
1 small tomato, chopped
1 small onion, chopped
2 tsp ground cumin

1 tsp salt
1 tbsp vegetable oil
2 small yellow potatoes, cubed

Directions

1. In a pan, mix together the lentils, water, tomato, onion, cumin, salt and vegetable oil on medium heat and bring to a boil.
2. Cook for about 30 minutes.
3. Add the potatoes and cook for about 15 minutes.

Whole Chicken
Colombian Style

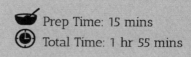 Prep Time: 15 mins

Total Time: 1 hr 55 mins

Servings per Recipe: 6

Calories	429 kcal
Fat	27.6 g
Cholesterol	13.8g
Sodium	32 g
Carbohydrates	97 mg
Protein	576 mg

Ingredients

1 (3 lb.) whole chicken, cut into pieces
1 lemon, juiced
1/4 C. olive oil
1 tsp salt
1/2 tsp ground black pepper
3/4 tsp paprika
1 (2.25 oz.) can sliced black olives, drained

1 large onion, chopped
1 medium green bell pepper, sliced
1 medium red bell pepper, sliced
1 1/2 C. orange juice

Directions

1. In a bowl, add the chicken pieces and drizzle with the lemon juice.
2. Refrigerate, covered for at least 30 minutes.
3. Set your oven to 350 degrees F.
4. In a small bowl, mix together the salt, pepper and paprika.
5. Sprinkle the spice mixture over the chicken pieces evenly.
6. In a skillet, heat the olive oil on medium-high heat and sear the chicken pieces till browned from both sides.
7. Transfer the chicken pieces into a baking dish and top with the olives, onion, green bell pepper and red bell pepper evenly.
8. Place the orange juice on top evenly.
9. With a piece of the foil, cover the baking dish and cook in the oven for about 45 minutes.

SPICY
Mexican Quinoa

Prep Time: 20 mins
Total Time: 40 mins

Servings per Recipe: 4
Calories	244 kcal
Fat	6.1 g
Carbohydrates	38.1g
Protein	8.1 g
Cholesterol	2 mg
Sodium	986 mg

Ingredients

1 tbsp olive oil
1 C. quinoa, rinsed
1 small onion, chopped
2 cloves garlic, minced
1 jalapeno pepper, seeded and chopped
1 (10 oz.) can diced tomatoes with
green chili peppers

1 envelope taco seasoning mix
2 C. low-sodium chicken broth
1/4 C. chopped fresh cilantro

Directions

1. In a large skillet, heat the oil on medium heat and stir fry the quinoa and onion for about 5 minutes.
2. Add the garlic and jalapeño pepper and cook for about 1-2 minutes.
3. Stir in the undrained can of diced tomatoes with green chilis, taco seasoning mix and chicken broth and bring to a boil.
4. Reduce the heat to medium-low and simmer for about 15-20 minutes.
5. Stir in cilantro and serve.

South
of the Border Style
Pesto

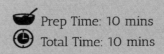 Prep Time: 10 mins

Total Time: 10 mins

Servings per Recipe: 6
Calories   176 kcal
Fat   17.8 g
Cholesterol   2.4g
Sodium   2.9 g
Carbohydrates   6 mg
Protein   262 mg

Ingredients

1/4 C. hulled pumpkin seeds (pepitas)
1 bunch cilantro
1/4 C. grated cotija cheese
4 cloves garlic
1 serrano chili pepper, seeded

1/2 tsp salt
6 tbsp olive oil

Directions

1. In a food processor, add the pumpkin seeds and pulse till chopped roughly.
2. Add the remaining ingredients and pulse till smooth.

EL POLLO
Soup

Prep Time: 20 mins
Total Time: 1 hr 5 mins

Servings per Recipe: 4
Calories	335 kcal
Fat	7.7 g
Carbohydrates	37.7g
Protein	31.5 g
Cholesterol	62 mg
Sodium	841 mg

Ingredients

3 cooked, boneless chicken breast halves, shredded
1 (15 oz.) can kidney beans
1 C. whole kernel corn
1 (14.5 oz.) can stewed tomatoes
1/2 C. chopped onion
1/2 green bell pepper, chopped

1/2 red bell pepper, chopped
1 (4 oz.) can chopped green chili peppers
2 (14.5 oz.) cans chicken broth
1 tbsp ground cumin

Directions

1. In a large pan mix together all the ingredients on medium heat.
2. Simmer for about 45 minutes.

Restaurant-Style
Latin Rice

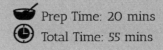 Prep Time: 20 mins

Total Time: 55 mins

Servings per Recipe: 6	
Calories	510 kcal
Fat	18.3 g
Carbohydrates	59.1g
Protein	28.3 g
Cholesterol	74 mg
Sodium	1294 mg

Ingredients

1 lb. lean ground beef
1 onion, diced
1 green bell pepper, diced
1 (14 oz.) can beef broth
2 C. fresh corn kernels
1 (10 oz.) can diced tomatoes with green chili peppers
1 (15 oz.) can tomato sauce
1/2 C. salsa

1/2 tsp chili powder
1/2 tsp paprika
1/2 tsp garlic powder
1/2 tsp salt
1/2 tsp ground black pepper
1 tsp minced cilantro
1 1/2 C. uncooked white rice
1 C. shredded Cheddar cheese

Directions

1. Heat a medium pan on medium heat and cook the beef till browned completely.
2. Drain off the grease from the pan.
3. Add the onion and green pepper and cook till the onion becomes tender.
4. Stir in the beef broth, corn, tomatoes with green chili peppers and tomato sauce, salsa, chili powder, paprika, garlic powder, salt, pepper and cilantro and bring to a boil.
5. Stir in the rice and cook, covered for about 25 minutes.
6. Top with the Cheddar cheese and cook for about 10 minutes.

CANELA
Brownies

Prep Time: 20 mins
Total Time: 1 hr 10 mins

Servings per Recipe: 30
Calories   206 kcal
Fat   10.8 g
Carbohydrates   27g
Protein   2.7 g
Cholesterol   62 mg
Sodium   76 mg

Ingredients

1 1/2 C. unsalted butter
3 C. white sugar
6 eggs
1 tbsp vanilla extract
1 1/4 C. unsweetened cocoa powder
1 3/4 tsp ground Mexican cinnamon
(canela)

1 1/2 C. all-purpose flour
1/2 tsp ground pequin chili pepper
3/4 tsp kosher salt
3/4 tsp baking powder

Directions

1. Set your oven to 350 degrees F before doing anything else and line a 15x12-inch baking dish with the parchment paper, leaving about 3 inches of paper overhanging 2 sides to use as handles.
2. In a microwave-safe bowl, add the butter and microwave on Medium for about 1 minute.
3. Add the sugar and mix till well combined.
4. Add the eggs, one at a time, and mix till well combined.
5. Stir in the vanilla extract.
6. In a bowl, sift together the flour, cocoa, cinnamon, pequin pepper, salt and baking powder.
7. Add the flour mixture into the butter mixture and mix till well combined.
8. Transfer the mixture into the prepared baking dish evenly.
9. Cook in the oven for about 20-25 minutes or till a toothpick inserted into the center comes out clean.
10. Remove from the oven and keep aside to cool in the pan.
11. Remove the parchment paper handles to remove the brownies for slicing.

Ground Beef
Mexican Dip

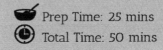 Prep Time: 25 mins

Total Time: 50 mins

Servings per Recipe: 32

Calories	150 kcal
Fat	11.3 g
Carbohydrates	3.9g
Protein	8.3 g
Cholesterol	30 mg
Sodium	429 mg

Ingredients

1 lb. ground beef
1 (16 oz.) jar salsa
1 (10.75 oz.) can condensed cream of
mushroom soup

2 lb. processed cheese food, cubed

Directions

1. Heat a medium pan on medium-high heat and cook the beef till browned completely.
2. Drain off the grease from the pan.
3. In a slow cooker, transfer the cooked beef with the salsa, condensed cream of mushroom soup and processed cheese food.
4. Set the slow cooker on High till cheese melts completely.
5. Now, set the slow cooker on Low and simmer till serving.

A STRONG COFFEE
in Mexico

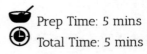
Prep Time: 5 mins
Total Time: 5 mins

Servings per Recipe: 32
Calories	150 kcal
Fat	11.3 g
Cholesterol	3.9 g
Sodium	8.3 g
Carbohydrates	30 mg
Protein	429 mg

Ingredients

1 sugar cube
1 fluid oz. hot water
3/4 C. coffee
1 fluid oz. coffee-flavored liqueur

1 tbsp whipped cream

Directions

1. In a coffee mug, add the sugar and hot water.
2. Stir in the coffee and liqueur and top with the whipped cream.

Quick
Midweek Mexican Macaroni

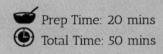 Prep Time: 20 mins

Total Time: 50 mins

Servings per Recipe: 8

Calories	374 kcal
Fat	21.4 g
Carbohydrates	23.5g
Protein	22.9 g
Cholesterol	79 mg
Sodium	997 mg

Ingredients

1 C. dry macaroni
1 lb. ground beef
1 small onion, chopped
1 (11 oz.) can whole kernel corn, drained

1 (10 oz.) can diced tomatoes with green chili peppers, drained
1 (1 lb.) loaf processed cheese, cubed

Directions

1. In large pan of the boiling water, add the macaroni for about 8 minutes.
2. Drain well.
3. Meanwhile, heat a medium skillet on medium-high heat and cook the beef till browned completely.
4. Add the onion and cook till browned.
5. Drain off the grease from the skillet.
6. Reduce the heat to medium and stir in the corn, tomatoes, cheese and cooked noodles.
7. Cook, stirring gently till bubbly.

BAKED
Banana Brazilian Style

Prep Time: 15 mins
Total Time: 30 mins

Servings per Recipe: 12	
Calories	135 kcal
Fat	3.9 g
Carbohydrates	26.2g
Protein	0.9 g
Cholesterol	5 mg
Sodium	56 mg

Ingredients

6 medium bananas, halved lengthwise
1/2 C. fresh orange juice
1 tbsp fresh lemon juice
1/2 C. white sugar

1/8 tsp salt
2 tbsp butter
1 C. flaked coconut

Directions

1. Set your oven to 400 degrees F before doing anything else and grease a 13x9-inch baking dish.
2. In a baking dish, place the bananas.
3. In a bowl, mix together the orange juice, lemon juice, sugar and salt.
4. Place the juice mixture over the bananas and top with the butter in the shape of dots.
5. Cook in the oven for about 15 minutes.
6. Serve with a sprinkling of the coconut.

Printed in Great Britain
by Amazon

29582480R00037